Contents

1	THE TRAMP	5
2	EARLY YEARS	9
3	THE WORKHOUSE	13
4	THE WICKED STEPMOTHER	19
5	A BRIEF SUCCESS	24
6	ON THE ROAD	31
7	CATTLEBOAT TO AMERICA	36
8	GOODBYE VAUDEVILLE	40
9	AMERICA LOVES CHARLIE	45
10	SCRAPS, THE TRAMP AND THE KID	51
11	THE END OF AN ERA	59
12	THE TRAMP MEETS THE QUEEN	63

1 The Tramp

As usual, when a film was being made, there was a lot of noise and confusion. People were hurrying everywhere, tripping over wires, shouting at each other, fiddling nervously with their costumes. They were making a Keystone Kops movie, called *Kids' Auto Races in Venice*. It was about children racing in wooden cars, surrounded by spectators and policemen. It was also supposed to be very funny.

The director's name was Mack Sennett. Mack was sitting with his head buried in his hands, wondering what he should do to make the film even funnier. Like all the others being made at that time, *Kids' Auto Races in Venice* was a silent movie. The talking film hadn't been invented yet. So all the humour had to come from what the actors did instead of what they said, and it was getting harder and harder to come up with new ideas. This was the trouble with all the Keystone Kops movies: all the jokes had been done before. Mack needed something fresh.

He looked up and saw, sitting in a corner, the pale, shy young Englishman he had hired as an actor. So far the Englishman hadn't been able to do anything right. He was very funny on the stage, but too stiff for films —

particularly the Keystone Kops type. Perhaps if he let him do exactly what he wanted, he would raise a laugh or two . . . . .

Mack called out through his megaphone. 'Chaplin! We need some gags here. Put on a comedy makeup. Anything will do.'

The Englishman jumped at hearing his name. He looked a little confused for a moment, then nodded and hurried to the dressing-room. He was gone ten minutes, and when he reappeared Mack Sennett and all the other people on the set stared in astonishment. Then they burst out laughing. They had never seen anything so ridiculous in their lives.

For the Englishman had put on a pair of baggy pants that were four times too big, a coat that was three times too small, shoes that were four times too big, and a derby hat that looked absurdly small perched on top of his curly hair. He had powdered his face heavily, so that his eyes stared out sadly, and had pasted a toothbrush moustache on his upper lip. He carried a cane which he whipped around as if it was alive. And he didn't walk: he shuffled, his feet pointing in opposite directions. He looked just like a tramp — who had once been a gentleman.

When filming started again the tramp shuffled into the action, interfering with everyone and attracting attention to himself. The cops were trying to keep everyone behind the fence, but the tramp insisted on walking in the middle of the racetrack, dodging the cars as they went zooming past him. When the cops tried to stop him he darted out of the way and hit one

on the backside with his cane. They chased him but he escaped and, from a safe distance away, pretended to walk like a flat-footed cop. He tripped over his feet. He tripped over cars. He tripped over cops. He looked worried and happy and angry — all at the same time. But he did everything so gracefully . . . . . and he made people laugh. How Mack Sennett, the cameraman and all the other people on the set roared with laughter!

That was how a legend was born. Charlie Chaplin, The Tramp, a gentleman, a poet, a dreamer, a lonely fellow, always hopeful of romance and adventure. A man who made eighty-six films in sixty years and made millions of people laugh until they cried. This is the story of Charlie Chaplin, the funniest man who ever lived.

2 Early Years

Charles Spencer Chaplin was born in Walworth, London, on 16 April 1889. His mother, Hannah, was a dainty lady with a beautiful voice, and was a popular singer and dancer. His father, who was also called Charles, worked on the stage too, but he drank rather a lot and soon after Charlie was born he deserted his family. Charlie had a brother, Sydney, who was four years older.

For the first five years of his life Charlie lived with Hannah and Sydney in three rooms in Lambeth. Hannah was much in demand on the stage at this time and made enough money to keep her little family in some comfort. One of Charlie's earliest memories was that each night before Hannah went to work he was tucked up in bed and left in the care of a housemaid, and when she came home Hannah would leave little presents of sweets and cakes on the table for the boys to eat in the morning — on the condition that they were very quiet as she liked to sleep late.

They lived quietly. On Sundays Hannah would dress Sydney in an Eton suit and Charlie in a blue velvet suit, and they would go for excursions along the Kennington Road. They would ride on horse-drawn trams, sitting upstairs and trying to touch passing lilac-trees, and would buy fruit and flowers from the market on the corner of Westminster Bridge. Sometimes they would go to museums and music-halls, where Charlie remembered being terrified to see a lady's head in a box surrounded by flames — and as the flames ate away at the wood of the box the head was smiling . . . . .

Charlie's earliest contact with the theatre and show-business came almost before he could speak. On weekdays, after Hannah woke up, she would teach Charlie and Sydney little songs from popular shows and would tell them all the latest gossip from the theatre. She was also very observant. She would stand by the window for hours, looking down at the street, and would keep the boys in fits by imitating the behaviour of the people down there. 'Oh, there goes Bill Smith!' she would exclaim. 'He's dragging his feet and his shoes are polished. He looks mad. I bet he's had a fight with his wife and she's sent him out without any breakfast. Look! He's going into that coffee shop for a roll!' Then she would act out the fight Bill Smith had had with his wife, making it look so silly that the boys would roll around on the floor in laughter, clutching at their stomachs.

Charlie said later that if it had not been for his mother he would have been a very ordinary performer. It was through watching her that he learned how to express emotion with his hands and his face, and how to observe and study people.

Then, when Charlie was five years old, something happened which was to change their lives completely.

Hannah had a sweet voice, but it wasn't very strong. She had to work hard, sometimes giving two or three performances a night, and her voice began to crack. One night she brought Charlie to the theatre to watch her sing. She was on stage when her voice suddenly dropped to a whisper. The audience began to laugh and make catcalls. The noise became so great that Hannah had to flee from the stage. She was very upset and the manager was extremely angry, saying that if she did not sing he wouldn't pay her. Then he noticed Charlie. He knew that the little boy could sing, and decided to let him take his mother's place on the stage. After a few words to the audience he told Charlie to sing.

Charlie was a very shy boy and terrified by the glare of the footlights and faces and smoke, but even at the age of five he knew how to catch an audience's attention. He began to sing a rather mischievous song called 'Jack Jones', about a rogue who had inherited a fortune and become very hoity-toity. The orchestra picked up his shrill voice and the audience loved it. Before Charlie had finished the song they began to throw money onto the stage. Immediately Charlie stopped singing and announced that he would pick up the money first and *then* continue singing. The audience roared at this and howled when the manager came onto the stage to help Charlie collect the money: the little boy thought that he was going to steal it and yelled with rage. When the confusion subsided Charlie continued singing, and when he had finished the audience clapped and whistled in appreciation.

That night was Charlie's first appearance on the stage and his mother's last.

3 The Workhouse

Hannah never regained her voice. She had saved a little money but soon it was all spent and they had to move from the comfort of their three rooms to a single, dark room in Oakley Street, just off the Kennington Road. Hannah pawned all her jewellery, and that kept the family going for a little longer; but when the money from that was gone and her voice had still not returned, she had to find other work. She was quick and clever with her hands and got a job sewing clothes.

It was very hard work for very little money. For the next two years life was a constant struggle. Often they didn't know where their next meal was coming from and for weeks at a time Charlie had to live on bread and dripping. Sydney had started going to school and in the evenings he sold newspapers, which helped a little. Then Hannah fell ill and couldn't work any longer. Their situation was becoming desperate when, one evening, Sydney came hurrying into the room with a purse he had found on the ground. It contained seven gold sovereigns and some silver — an absolute fortune. The purse must have belonged to an extremely rich person, but there was no name or address on it, so Hannah couldn't return it. It seemed like a godsend.

Hannah used the money to buy new clothes for Charlie and Sydney, and there was enough left over to take a short holiday in Southend. In the sea air Hannah recovered her health and Charlie grew brown and happy; but the holiday ended all too soon and they had to return to their one room in London.

Hard times again befell them. Like sand in an hour-glass, their money ran out, and the crisis came when Hannah's sewing machine was taken away in payment of the grocer's bill. There was now no alternative. In 1896, when Charlie was seven years old, he entered the Lambeth Workhouse with his mother and brother.

Victorian workhouses were ghastly places where all your belongings were taken away from you and you were forced to do the most degrading work for your keep. Families were also split up and it wasn't long before Charlie and Sydney were separated from their mother and sent to the Hanwell School for Orphans and Destitute Children, about twenty kilometres out of London. Now Sydney was sent to live with the senior boys and Charlie with the juniors, so that for the first time in his life Charlie had no member of his family close by to talk to and play with.

At first Charlie was miserable, for he was very shy and found it difficult to make friends. Soon, however, he started going to school and the novelty of learning how to read and write distracted him. The school was very strict. It was run along military lines, and the punishment for the smallest offence was a savage caning. Every Friday morning all three hundred boys

who attended the school marched into the gymnasium and formed three sides of a square. On the fourth side, behind a long table, stood the boys who were to be punished that day. One by one they would be laid across the table and beaten with a cane that was as thick as a man's thumb and about a metre long. It was terrifying to watch.

One Thursday Charlie was astonished to hear his name being called out for punishment the next day. He was accused of having set fire to the *lavatories*, of all places. Charlie was too frightened to protest his innocence and was caned three times. The pain was terrible: so bad he couldn't breathe and couldn't move for twenty minutes. He had to be carried to a mattress to recover. Sydney was very angry when he heard about the caning, but there was little he could do. Secretly, however, Charlie felt proud of himself that he hadn't cried out.

Soon after that Sydney had his eleventh birthday. At this age a workhouse boy had the choice of joining the army or the navy, and he decided to join the navy. Now Charlie was more alone than ever.

Finally, after what seemed like an eternity to the little boy, Hannah found another job and was able to take Charlie away from Hanwell. Sydney promptly left the navy to rejoin them and for a while they were able to live on the money Hannah was making. But it wasn't long before things got much worse. First Hannah fell very ill again, and the two boys had to go back to the workhouse; and then one day two nurses called Sydney away to tell him that his mother had gone insane. Hannah's sickness and near-starvation had done terrible things to her mind, so that she didn't know who

she was any longer. For her own safety she had been sent to the Cane Hill Lunatic Asylum. Charlie said later that it felt as if the world had fallen in on him. Why had she done this? Mother, so light-hearted and gay, how could she go insane? He didn't cry: he couldn't, but a baffling despair overcame him.

There was one small compensation, however. The court decided that Sydney and Charlie were to live with their father until Hannah recovered. Charlie hadn't seen his father for years, so that was something to look forward to; at least it meant that he would be leaving the workhouse for good. And he didn't want to go back — ever.

4 The Wicked Stepmother

Charlie and Sydney arrived at their father's home in a bread van. They were met by his second wife, Louise. She had once been an attractive woman but constant drinking had coarsened her appearance and now she looked haggard and sad.

Louise had a young son of her own, and deeply resented having her husband's children by his earlier marriage staying at her house. Right from the start she did her best to make Charlie's and Sydney's lives miserable. She was so unpleasant to Sydney that he began to spend as much time as possible away from the house, and Charlie was made to do all sorts of housework as soon as he came home from school. He was lucky: Louise merely resented him, but she hated Sydney, calling him a little swine who should be sent to a reformatory.

At least Charlie got to know his father. He was fascinated by him and began to copy many of his gestures: the way he ate, and moved his hands, for example. Unfortunately he was still drinking far too much, and would often reel home, his face ghostly pale, unable to say a word. Louise also drank constantly, and when drunk would usually sit and brood, staring

into space, mumbling to herself. Or she would scream at the unhappy Charlie, who would sit in a corner of the room, trying to make himself invisible. He said later that the nights he spent in that house with only a drunk Louise for company were the longest and saddest of his life.

One afternoon Charlie got home from school to find the house locked up. Louise had gone out and forgotten about him. He couldn't get into the house and couldn't have any lunch. He was relieved, however, at least he wouldn't have to wash floors or chop wood or clean the house . . . . But as the afternoon wore on and became evening, and evening turned into night, Charlie grew worried. Sydney was not around. He hated living with Louise so much that he would often disappear for a few days. Sitting on the front steps, Charlie was tired and hungry, and afraid that he had been abandoned. He wandered around, looking into cafe windows and shops, and was nearly in despair. He eventually returned home, but the door was still locked and the house in darkness. Finally, close to midnight, he saw a figure staggering down the street. He recognised it at once. It was Louise, and she was very drunk. As she approached Charlie ran up to her in relief. She brushed him aside as if he was a fly. 'You're not my son, you're not coming into my home!' she shrieked as she went inside, slamming the door in his face.

Charlie didn't know what to do. He didn't know where Sydney was: for all he knew his brother had already been thrown out of the house. And as for his father . . . . where *was* he? Suddenly he remembered that after a performance his father often drank at a pub some distance away. Perhaps he was still there, or Charlie could catch him on his way home.

So Charlie started running towards the pub. It was cold and dark and he was scared — eventually he saw his father's shadowy figure coming towards him, outlined by the street lamps. He was also quite drunk, and he was surprised to be met by his son so late at night. When he heard what Louise had done he was furious. He caught hold of Charlie's hand and hurried him home. As soon as he came in through the door he picked up a heavy clothes-brush and threw it at Louise, hitting her on the side of the face. She collapsed on the floor unconscious.

After this Louise's hatred for the boys could not be masked. Every time she knew that their father was going to be away for the night she threw them out of the house, and they had to spend the nights sleeping under bridges and in doorways. They would huddle together for warmth and sleep with one eye open virtually all the time on the lookout for tramps and drunks.

Charlie soon grew accustomed to this existence. He was glad that Sydney stayed with him and took care of him, and that he didn't have to face Louise's drunken rages alone. In a curious way he even enjoyed the adventure of sleeping in the street like a vagabond.

At last, to Charlie's joy, Hannah was discharged from hospital. She immediately took the boys away, and they moved to a small room at 3 Pownall Terrace. For the first time in a long while Charlie was really happy. He, Sydney and his mother were together again. Hannah's

health was good and they had enough money to live on. Moreover, Charlie was beginning to enjoy school. From having been a shy and obscure little boy he began to blossom, using his developing skills at mimicry to make the other boys laugh, and endearing himself to his teachers with his quick brain.

Then, when Charlie was only nine years old, his father during one of his rare visits suggested that it was about time Charlie started thinking about a career on the stage. He had just the opening for him: Mr Jackson had asked him if he could find a boy for his troupe of clog dancers, the Eight Lancashire Lads. Hannah was reluctant to let Charlie go at first, but when her husband pointed out that it would be a great help financially, she agreed. So Charlie left school and began his professional career as a clog dancer — for half-a-crown a week and his lodging.

5 A Brief Success

Mr Jackson's clog dancers were just that: eight little boys and girls who would patter out onto the stage and dance in wooden shoes as a warm-up act — getting the audience ready for the main attractions. They were very popular, partly because they were so professional — Mr Jackson made sure that they practised very hard — but also because they looked so fresh and rosy-cheeked. They would also occasionally act in pantomimes.

It took Charlie six weeks to learn how to dance, and the skill he acquired became as natural to him as walking. The Eight Lancashire Lads went from town to town in England, never staying more than a week in each place, and Charlie enjoyed himself immensely in the company of the other boys and girls. They treated him as one of the family and gradually he lost his shyness. Sometimes he longed for his mother and Sydney, but the work and constant travelling occupied him most of the time. The training he got was to last him for the rest of his life. After an initial period of stage-fright, when he found it almost impossible to move his feet in front of an audience, he became quite accustomed to being on stage. He learned how to use

his feet and body to show mood and emotion, and gradually he began to realise that he had a gift for making people laugh.

The first time he consciously set out to make people laugh at his antics was when the Eight Lancashire Lads were playing in London as a supporting act for the great clown Marceline. Charlie was given a small part in one of Marceline's sketches. It was a kitchen scene, and Charlie played a cat with a surprised look on its face. The idea was that he would be drinking milk and Marceline would trip over him — again and again. This went well a couple of times and the audience laughed heartily. Then Charlie decided to add some bits of his own.

The next time, instead of going straight to his saucer of milk, Charlie darted up to one of the other children who was playing a dog, and sniffed energetically at the dog's rear end. The audience roared with laughter. Charlie turned to them and winked; then he sniffed again. Delighted with the laughter, he padded over to one of the curtains, sniffed and, quite unlike a cat, lifted his leg. The audience exploded. The stage manager ran onto the stage and hustled Charlie off while the audience was applauding him, and gave the little boy a serious talking-to. In those days there were very strict rules about what could be performed in public and this was the sort of thing that would get the show closed by the Lord Chamberlain. But Charlie's ambition had been stirred: there was now nothing he would rather do than make people laugh.

For the next six months Charlie was very happy. The work and regular food put a flush in his cheeks and a sparkle in his eye: he was still small for his age, but was developing the confidence of a man. The Eight Lancashire Lads took part in shows with many of the leading entertainers of the day, and Charlie learned a little from every one of them. He might have gone on to become one of the most famous music hall performers of all time when suddenly disaster struck.

Charlie began to have difficulty breathing. It got so bad that he couldn't go on stage any longer and had to spend hours lying in bed. The doctors said that he had asthma: not very serious and something he would grow out of, but in the meantime he couldn't work . . . . Mr Jackson immediately sent him back to Hannah.

Once he was at home and in his mother's care, Charlie's health improved. Before too long his asthma had nearly disappeared, but Hannah was reluctant to send him back to the music hall. Her career on stage had harmed her health and she didn't want the same thing to happen to him. So, not for the first time, Charlie found himself back in the twilight world of poverty.

His father died in 1901, at the age of thirty-seven, from drinking too much. Sydney was trying to find a job, and Hannah was working terribly hard sewing clothes for one shilling and sixpence. This would be about seven and a half pence a day. In those days it was just enough for a loaf of bread and a piece of meat.

Charlie was twelve by now. He decided that he would have to leave school and try to make some money to help out. He sold flowers without much success, and tried to sell the family's old clothes: all he got rid of was a pair of sad-looking gaiters — for sixpence. He became an errand boy for a week. Then a doctor's boy, until the doctor decided that he was too young for the job. He became a page in a large house in Lancaster Gate, until his sense of humour got him into trouble and he was fired. Then he worked on a printing press washing ink off enormous rollers which weighed forty five kilograms each . . . . more than his own body weight. This was a filthy, back-breaking job, with ink splashing onto his clothes. He was constantly getting his fingers caught in the machinery — and it was finally too much for the boy. He came down with influenza, and when he had recovered Hannah insisted that he return to school. She would make ends meet without his help.

Meanwhile Sydney had got himself a job as a bugler on a ship bound for Africa. It was a wonderful, romantic job, and every time he came back to London he would give his wages to his mother. It wasn't very much money, but it was enough to keep Hannah and Charlie going for a while; unfortunately it always ran out a week or two weeks before Sydney returned to London from another voyage. Then Hannah would have to work twice as hard, and there would be days when there wasn't a thing to eat.

Hannah had another breakdown during one of these bad times — the most serious one yet. She had to go back to the Cane Hill Asylum. Charlie was now in a desperate plight. Sydney was somewhere at sea, there was no money and he couldn't find a job. He didn't want to go back to the workhouse, not ever. For a while Charlie stayed in the room, stealing out at night to find scraps of food but almost starving. Then he managed to persuade some wood-choppers to give him a job — for tuppence a day — and he managed to survive until Sydney came home.

When Sydney returned to London this time he was almost rich. On the voyage to Africa he had organised sweepstakes and lotteries, and had made forty pounds. That was a lot of money in those days — enough to keep the family in comfort for six months at least. He was horrified to see his brother starving and living like a frightened animal, and decided that he would give up his job to be with him. He thought that because of their family's connections they would both be able to find jobs on the stage, and once he had outfitted Charlie with new clothes they began to do the rounds of the theatrical agents.

It was not long, once the decision to make a career on the stage had been made, before the Chaplin brothers found regular work. The tragedy was that in the years that followed Hannah was never really able to enjoy her sons' success. She never recovered completely. The long years of suffering had destroyed her mind, and she remained in care for the rest of her life.

6 On the Road

Charlie already had a bit of a reputation. Many theatre people knew his parents and one or two influential critics had heard of his performance with the Eight Lancashire Lads — particularly his triumph with Marceline. With Sydney's help it didn't take long to find a play to act in. Charlie's first important part was in a play called *From Rags to Riches*. It was a terrible play, but he made the most of it. At this time the music hall and playhouse were the major entertainments: cinema and television had not been invented yet. As a result, although *From Rags to Riches* was awful, it still played to large audiences all over England. Charlie was a leading actor in it, and he learned how to perfect his skills on stage.

When this play ended he was offered a part in *Jim: A Romance of Cockayne*. This was another disastrous play, but it opened at the Drury Lane Theatre, one of the most important in London. The play was a flop — it lasted just one night — but the critics singled Charlie out for the quality of his acting. It was the first time his name had appeared in print and gave Charlie a taste of the success that was to follow. One newspaper said, 'Master Charlie Chaplin is a broth of a boy, giving a

31

most realistic picture of the cheeky, honest, loyal, self-reliant, philosophic street Arab.'

Because of this one performance, Charlie was given his best part yet. One of the most famous actors in England was a man called William Gillette, and he was the star in a play called *Sherlock Holmes*. Charlie was cast as Billy, Sherlock Holmes' page-boy, and his performance once more attracted compliments.

Charlie was now firmly established as an actor. He was in great demand and was making a lot of money. His days of poverty were behind him, but he never forgot them. He also didn't forget that he wanted to make people laugh, and he got the opportunity to do this very soon in a vaudeville show called *The Casey Circus*.

The show was made up of a number of sketches, and as usual Charlie had a starring part. In one of the sketches he impersonated a very popular doctor of the day who had the reputation of being a crook as well as a gentleman. The audience recognised him immediately, and Charlie was a howling success. His impersonation was so funny that for a long time afterwards the real doctor was the laughing-stock of London. And Charlie had discovered the secret of making people laugh. It was all a question of timing and of being able to surprise people. For example, he would walk onto the stage as a serious, dignified man, dressed very properly in a morning coat with tails. He would stand in front of the audience, striking a dramatic pose, every inch of him looking important. Then he would stride towards an easy chair, spread his coat-tails with an elegant gesture

— and plonk himself down on the cat! It worked every time.

Charlie was still only seventeen when one of the biggest boosts to his career took place. Sydney was working for a director called Fred Karno, a man who had done more than any other to make pantomime and comedy a world-wide entertainment. Sydney persuaded Karno to try Charlie out. Because Karno set such high standards for comedy, Charlie had to work harder for him than ever before. Not for Karno the cheerful, direct comedy Charlie was used to playing: Karno demanded subtlety and thoughtfulness. The audience had to be made to laugh until they cried; then they had to be made to cry until they laughed again. The actor had to be in complete control at all times.

Charlie was quick to learn this new type of comedy,

and when he started appearing he was an immediate sensation.

He developed such a talent for combining Karno's brand of comedy with his own sense of humour that every time he appeared on stage the audience was delighted. One sketch in particular made them explode. It was called *The Mumming Birds,* and in it Charlie played a drunken member of the audience watching a very bad play. His antics — falling off his chair onto the stage, shrieking in agony whenever the acting got too bad, pelting the worst actors with fruit, falling asleep and waking with a start and a shout — kept everyone in stitches.

Charlie's first three years with Karno were extremely important. From being just a very talented performer he became a professional whose type of humour was unique. Comedy cannot be rigid. It is an art and has to change all the time, adapting itself to a particular audience and a specific mood. To be a great comedian you have to learn how to change. Charlie learned. More than that, he developed a very clear idea of what good comedy was, and as his experience grew so did his artistry: by 1910, at the age of twenty-one, he was probably the most accomplished comedian in the British Isles. Now he wanted to be the best in the world.

7 Cattleboat to America

To be the best comedian in the world meant being the best in America, which was fast becoming the centre of the entertainment world. So Charlie was delighted to learn that he would be touring the States with Karno's company. By that time it had become clear that Charlie had done all that a comedian could in England.

So in September 1910 the company sailed on the SS *Cairnrona*, bound for New York. The ship was a cattle-boat, and Charlie and the others felt a little like cattle too: the boat was so overcrowded with immigrants and the food was terrible. But the passengers didn't mind. Most of them were very poor and were hoping that America would offer them a new and better life.

A couple of weeks later the ship entered New York Harbour. All the passengers crowded the rails to stare at the Statue of Liberty and the fabled New York skyline. Charlie, wearing his smartest suit and derby hat in celebration, leaned against the rail, drinking in his first view of America. And as the ship drifted past the Statue of Liberty the young man took off his hat with a flourish and announced, 'America, I have come to conquer you! Every man, woman and child will have

my name on their lips — Charles Spencer Chaplin!'

America did not disappoint him. Things happened much more quickly there — fortunes and reputations could be made in an instant, and new faces and ideas were greeted with open arms. The Karno company were welcomed right across America, and their performances were treated as events of some importance. Nearly every newspaper wrote about the tour, and the publicity was like a tonic to Charlie. He thrived on it.

The company travelled from town to town for twenty weeks, starting in New York and finishing in Salt Lake City, right in the heart of the continent. It was hard work: they had to give three performances a day, and Karno hadn't helped by insisting that the main sketch was to be a piece called *The Wow-Wows* — an extremely silly skit on secret societies. The company hated playing it, and American audiences were puzzled, not understanding the very English brand of humour. Nevertheless the tour was a triumph from beginning to end, and a good part of its success was due to Charlie himself. Most Americans thought him a remarkable comedian and his fellow troupe-members recognised that it was his talent that transformed them from moderately good to excellent.

As a result of their success the company was booked for a further six weeks in New York. It was there that Mack Sennett, who would soon start his own movie company, Keystone, first saw Charlie perform, and he was dazzled by the young man's grace. It was a sketch called *A Night in an English Music Hall* — an adaptation of *The Mumming Birds* — and Sennett said later that he 'was impressed. More than impressed. Stunned would be a good word. I think I was so struck by him because he was everything I wasn't: a little fellow who could move like a ballet dancer — and was funny besides!'

Another tour followed, twenty weeks cross-country to California. At the end of it the company sailed back to England, exhausted but happy. Charlie knew that he had done well. He was now convinced that his future lay in America. He liked the people: they seemed much more open and friendly than the English. In addition, his background — poverty and the slums of London — didn't seem to matter there. He was determined to return as soon as possible.

Back in London, Charlie resumed his normal routine with Karno's company. He was kept busy and lived comfortably, although occasionally he was lonely. So much travelling gave him little opportunity to make friends. His brother Sydney had recently got married and was absorbed in his new life. So Charlie was relieved when Karno arranged a second tour of America and asked him to head the cast. He packed up the few things he needed and gave away the rest of his belongings: in his mind he had already left London for good.

The last thing Charlie did before boarding the ship was to visit his mother. She lived in a rest-home and he was saddened to see how withdrawn she was — it took her a long time to recognise him. He made a promise to himself that he would send for her as soon as he was settled in America, and left the city of his birth with only a trace of regret.

Charlie kept his promise. But it was not until 1920 that his mother was able to travel to America, and she lived in comfort in California for the rest of her life.

8 Goodbye Vaudeville

Not too surprisingly, this new tour of the States was a bit of a letdown at first. Charlie had visited all the places before and America was less dazzling the second time around. Sightseeing in more remote areas was impossible because the tour was even more strenuous than the last. Moreover Charlie was worried by the prospect of finding the right sort of work.

A new form of entertainment had become popular — the moving picture — and cinemas had sprung up by the thousand all over America. Charlie saw as many films as he could. They were in black and white, of course, and without sound, but to audiences in 1913 they were magical. Charlie was fascinated. He sensed that once the cinema became firmly established the popularity of his brand of vaudeville and music-hall comedy would decline. Although he could have any vaudeville job he wanted in America, he knew that if he wanted to press on with his career his future lay in films.

Then he had a stroke of luck. Mack Sennett, who by now had set up his own company, Keystone, needed someone to replace one of his leading actors. He remembered seeing a wonderful English comedian in

A Night in an English Music Hall, but he couldn't remember his name! Something like Chaffin . . . .

So, on May 12, 1913, he sent a telegram to Philadelphia, where the Karno company was playing: IS THERE A MAN NAMED CHAFFIN IN YOUR COMPANY OR SOMETHING LIKE THAT STOP IF SO WILL HE COMMUNICATE WITH KESSEL AND BAUMAN 24 LONGACRE BUILDING BROADWAY NEW YORK

Since Charlie was the only person in the company with a name even vaguely like Chaffin he assumed that the telegram referred to him. Kessel and Bauman were Sennett's agents in New York, he discovered, and so went to see them straight away. Before he really knew it he had signed a contract for a year of filming, to start as soon as he finished the tour. Charlie Chaplin was now a movie actor.

To begin with he was not very successful. Charlie's

style of humour was very different from that of the Keystone Kops, his new colleagues. Also, he was used to having an audience in front of him and relied on their laughter to tell him if his timing and jokes were having effect. Working in front of a camera he really had no idea if what he was doing was funny. The Keystone comedies were quite different from anything he had done before. American film-makers had decided that the best recipe for comedy was a slapstick formula — lots of ridiculous chases, backside-kicking, daredevil stunts and exaggerated, clumsy gags. Charlie, on the other hand, was a much more sophisticated comedian. He could do anything the Keystone Kops could do, but the difference was Keystone humour meant slapping you in the face with jokes, while Charlie preferred to sneak up from behind and surprise you. Also, since this was the era of the silent movie, all the comedy had to come from what the actors *did*, not what they said. Up to then Charlie had been able to use both words and actions.

Mack Sennett, however, had the wisdom to allow Charlie to do what he wanted, and the Tramp, the most famous comedy creation of all time, was born. From that time on Charlie was a vital member of the Keystone Kops. He didn't always play a tramp, but, provided that he was allowed to, he injected new and funny elements into each film. In *Mabel's Strange Predicament,* for example, Charlie's third film, Mack Sennett simply asked him to be funny in a hotel. With complete grace and a serious expression Charlie proceeded to act like a *very* drunk drunk. He tripped over a dog, got his foot caught in an elevator, was surprised sleeping on a dining-table and was chased all over the hotel; Mack and the camera crew, who had seen a lot of funny things in their day, were in hysterics.

Unfortunately Charlie was not always allowed to do what he wanted. Many people were jealous of him and often his part in a film would be cut by unfriendly directors; so he delivered a warning to Mack. Either he be allowed to direct his *own* films, and so have some control over what went into them, or he would leave. Mack was aghast. He didn't know whether Charlie was capable of directing, but he didn't want to lose him: Charlie was without a doubt the funniest man in the company. Finally he agreed, provided that Charlie stuck to the formula which had worked for previous Keystone movies. It was a wise decision. There were immediate results in the area Mack was most interested in — the box-office. Reports filtered back from all over the country about the Chaplin films. His films were making twice as much money as anything else from Keystone.

One of Charlie's best films for Keystone was *Mabel's Married Life*. Again he played a drunk, and had a violent argument with a punching-bag which he thought had broken into his house. Another comedian doing the part would have imitated a drunk and staggered around, rolling his eyes and falling over things; it wouldn't have been very funny. Charlie, instead, like a *real* drunk, wandered around trying to look *sober*!

In that one year, 1914, Charlie made 35 short films for the Keystone studio. He directed most of them himself, and the ones he didn't were not as good. By the time his contract ended he was the biggest comedy star in America. Naturally Sennett wanted him to continue working at Keystone, but Charlie wanted greater control over his movies. Another studio offered him greater artistic freedom — and much more money — and he left Keystone.

9 America Loves Charlie

Charlie's new employers were the Essanay Film Manufacturing company, who had a studio in California. His talent flowered in the warm sun. When he went from Keystone to Essanay he was a very good comedian and director; by the time he left the studio in California — one year and 14 films later — he was a phenomenon.

By 1915 a Chaplin craze was sweeping America. Children wore Chaplin buttons and imitated his walk. Cinema-owners didn't bother to put his name up on the billboards any longer: they simply placed life-sized photographs of him outside their cinemas — everyone would know that a Chaplin film was showing. Songs were written about him. The First World War had just started, and soldiers in France sang as they marched:

The moon shines bright on Charlie Chaplin
   Whose boots are crackin'
   For want of blackin'
And his little baggy trousers
   They want mendin'
   Before we send 'im
To the Dardanelles!

The films he made at Essanay were the same length

as at Keystone. He was still experimenting and looking for new ways to use the camera — he had been making films for only two years! — and it was during this period that Charlie developed the character of The Tramp.

Charlie's first masterpiece was centred on this creation, and it was aptly called *The Tramp*. In it he played a wanderer who saved a pretty girl from robbers and was rewarded with a job on her father's farm. The Tramp was a total failure as a labourer. He dropped a sack of flour on the farmer's toes. With a pitchfork he was a menace to everyone, and he tried to milk a cow by pulling at her tail. He had many adventures, and saved the pretty girl a number of times from fates worse than death. In the end her fiancé reappeared and the Tramp had to leave the farm. The most wonderful scene in the movie came right at the end. The Tramp walked away, his shoulders drooping in despair, the picture of dejection. Then suddenly, he perked up. He whipped his cane elegantly, gave a little skip and walked briskly down the road. It was this optimism which became one of the best-loved aspects of the Tramp's character.

On the whole the films Charlie made that year were jolly affairs with a little sentimentality thrown in. But Charlie had a more serious side and felt an urge to expose some of the unfairness of life. His last film at Essanay was called *Police!*, and he played a convict who had just been released from prison. He had a number of adventures which were extremely funny but which also underlined how hard life was for people with criminal records. The humour reinforced the message, a combination that was to feature in many of his future films.

Charlie left Essanay at the end of 1915. He had enjoyed greater artistic freedom there than at Keystone, but his projects were becoming ever more ambitious, and there wasn't enough money to do the films he wanted. He moved to the Mutual Film Corporation, where he would have a huge budget for every film he made in addition to a salary of $10,000 a week! Charlie took a much-needed holiday, travelling by train from California to New York, and he was amazed by the evidence of his popularity. Huge crowds jammed every station along the route and the police were hard-pressed to control them. In the end Charlie was asked to get off the train before it reached New York. There was such a crush at Grand Central Station in that city that they were afraid people might be killed.

Charlie had come a long way from his poverty-stricken days in London. The success he was enjoying now was beyond his wildest dreams. But for some reason he felt depressed: perhaps he had come too far too quickly. It would have been a help if there had been a friend close by, but he had always been shy and still found friendships difficult. He cheered up, however, when he started making films for Mutual.

His greater financial freedom with Mutual allowed Charlie to devote more time to each film. He paid greater attention to sets and introduced jokes more cleverly. Social themes remained important and the comical and lovable Tramp became a stern critic of society.

Every film Charlie made for Mutual seemed to be funnier than the last one, but all had a serious side. For example *The Immigrant* was about very poor people going to America on a cattle-boat. In a series of very funny episodes they discovered that the New World could be both friendly and dangerous at the same time. It was a film close to Charlie's heart: he said later that of all the films he made *The Immigrant* touched him the most.

Charlie's funniest film during this period was *The Pawnshop*. It contains one of the most celebrated pieces of film comedy ever made — and it is still referred to as a perfect example of how to make people laugh. The Tramp is helping out in a pawnshop. A rather furtive man comes into the shop with an alarm-clock to pawn. Charlie has to examine it carefully, to make sure that it is working properly, and he starts by listening to it through a doctor's stethoscope. Then he attacks it with a hammer and drill, opens it up with a can-opener, sniffs at the contents and looks at it with a magnifying-glass. Then, with a pair of pliers, he pulls everything out from the inside and tries to oil the pieces as they dance around on the counter. Finally he sweeps the mess up into the client's hat and hands it back to him with a shrug — it's not really worth pawning . . .

Charlie made twelve films for Mutual between 1916 and 1917, and he said that this was one of the happiest periods of his life. He was not yet thirty years old, and already he had done more than most men could achieve in two lifetimes. He had also made a lot of money — by 1918 he was a millionaire. Yet his most important and productive time was still to come.

10 Scraps, The Tramp and the Kid

In 1917 Charlie started making films for First National. His unique creation, the Tramp, was now the best-known and most-loved personality in the world of entertainment. People all over the world were laughing at his antics. Everyone recognised his splayfooted, shuffling walk and quick, graceful hops out of danger. His cane was part of his body and what he did with it was a constant delight — whether it was prodding, clubbing, supporting or hooking; used as a toothpick or backscratcher, to trip up nasty people or to lift up ladies' skirts. Charlie's face was another weapon. It was grave most of the time, but everyone knew that when he twitched his mouth and arched his eyebrows he was about to do something wicked.

And he was still growing. In the next thirteen years Charlie made fifteen films featuring the Tramp in different roles, and every one of them was a masterpiece. During this time he moved from First National to United Artists, a company he set up himself with two partners, Douglas Fairbanks and Mary Pickford. He also returned to London in triumph and he revisited his old haunts.

Charlie's first film for National was a story about a

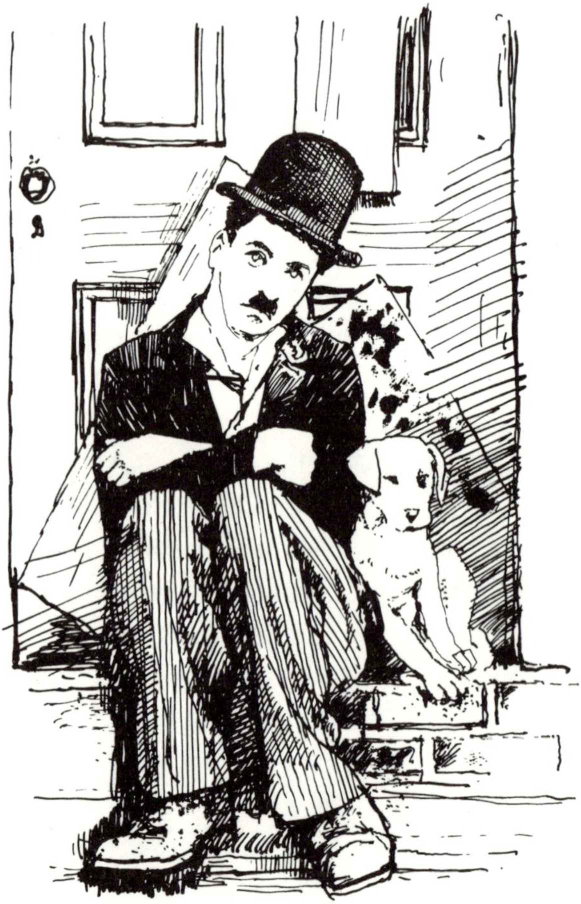

tramp and a dog, called *A Dog's Life*. In it Charlie befriended Scraps, a 'thoroughbred mongrel', and the two of them went into partnership to do the only things they knew how to do well — to steal food and annoy people. For example, Charlie stole a half-empty bottle of milk and offered to share it with Scraps; the dog examined the bottle and looked up at Charlie in puzzlement; he couldn't get his head into the neck. Charlie proceeded to show the dog how to manage it by dipping the dog's tail into the bottle and licking the milk off. In another scene Scraps stole a string of sausages from a roadside stall while Charlie distracted the owner, and the two of them escaped wolfing down the sausages while the angry owner and assorted policemen chased them. The film ended with Charlie and his sweetheart looking lovingly down into a baby's cot; the camera slowly took us from the faces of the happy couple to the object of their affection — in the cot is . . . . . Scraps . . . . with a litter of beautiful puppies. Scraps was female!

A Dog's Life was Charlie's most realistic film to date. The poverty that the tramp and the dog lived in was frightening, and Charlie wanted to show that conditions like that still existed in the United States. This film marked the start of his most brilliant period. It would be impossible to describe every film he made, but *The Kid* and *The Gold Rush* must get attention. These two films are still considered to be among the best comedies ever made.

The Kid was the story of a friendship between a tramp and a little boy who had been abandoned by his mother

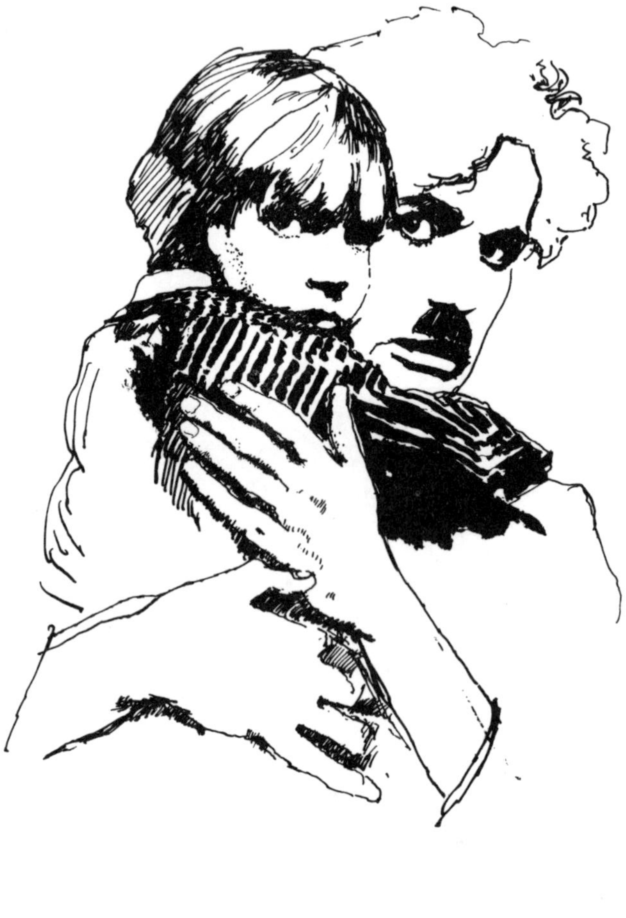

when he was a baby. Charlie came along, twirling his cane and dodging the rubbish being flung out of windows. He removed his gloves with great dignity, opened his cigarette-case, which just happened to be a converted sardine-tin, and took out a half-smoked cigarette. Then he saw the baby. With great care he carried him back to his dingy room, appointed himself nanny and proceeded to feed him from a teapot. Soon Jackie — the baby grown into a little boy — was helping Charlie in his line of business — breaking windows for Charlie to mend. Most of the film was concerned with Charlie and Jackie getting away from people who tried to separate them. It all ended happily when Jackie's mother, who had become a famous opera singer, finally tracked her son down and took him — and the Tramp — back to her mansion to live a life of comfort.

The Kid won tremendous praise. Very few people left the cinema without tears in their eyes — and no one could be sure that they were tears of happiness. It was, in fact, a very moving film. One critic said 'There is, at least for me, more emotion in a single tear of *The Kid* than in all the bucketfuls of opera . . . . I do not laugh at Charlie till I cry. I laugh *lest* I cry, which is a very different matter.'

The *Gold Rush* had the Tramp in a very Arctic region of the Yukon. It was an involved story about the discovery of an enormous goldfield and the hardships the miners went through. One of the best moments came when Charlie was trapped by the snow in an isolated cabin. There was no food to eat and the situation grew more desperate each day. He was faint

with hunger when suddenly a thought struck him. With great care and excitement he removed one of his shoes, placed it lovingly in a large pot filled with water, and boiled it gently. Then, like a master chef, he took a large knife to it and carved. The sole, like a succulent steak, he ate with fork and knife; then he curled the shoelaces around his fork like spaghetti and sucked at the nails in the shoe as if they were juicy chicken bones. No five-course dinner could have given more enjoyment to Charlie than this modest, bizarre meal.

Many critics think that *The Gold Rush* was the finest film Charlie ever made. Very recently, in fact, the International Film Jury rated it the second best film of all time. Put another way, *The Gold Rush* is the best *comedy* film of all time.

In 1921 Charlie returned to London for the first time in eleven years. No artist before or since has had the reception Charlie received when he got back to England. Hysteria gathered like a storm before his ship was half-way across the Atlantic. One newspaper reported: 'Chaplin returns like a conqueror! Progress from Southampton to London will resemble a Roman triumph.' The paper was right. Boats went out to sea to meet the ship, and when Charlie finally arrived at Waterloo Station in London he was greeted by a crowd that was like an ocean, spilling out of the station and blocking all the traffic on the surrounding roads. Nothing had prepared Charlie for such a reception. He was overwhelmed by so much love. And the frenzy continued. When he reached his room at the Ritz Hotel, he had to go to the window again and again to wave at the crowds below. It was hours before they finally left him in peace.

As soon as this happened Charlie hurriedly changed his clothes and left the hotel by a back door. He hailed a taxi and was off, down the Haymarket, over Westminster Bridge and, at last, the Kennington Road.

Charlie wandered around his childhood haunts for hours, reliving his past, remembering all the good (and bad) times. Everything seemed much greyer and smaller now, and the desolation of the neighbourhood weighed heavily. Finally he left, almost at a run: it felt as though those streets of poverty still had the power to trap him in their hopelessness.

11 The End of an Era

From 1931 to 1938, a year before the outbreak of the Second World War, Charlie made only three films. The era of the silent movie had finished and talking pictures had taken over. Charlie knew that one of the most important aspects of his art was the silence of the Tramp, and he felt that giving him a voice would destroy the magic. He made only two more films featuring the Tramp. The first was called *City Lights* and it was a classic among silent movies — this at a time when everyone else was making films with soundtracks. The magic was still there, however, and *City Lights* made more money for Charlie than any film before or after.

In his next film, *Modern Times*, which was a satire on the age of machinery, Charlie gave the Tramp a voice for the first time. But it is typical of his sense of humour that the Tramp did not say anything commonplace . . . .

In this film the Tramp had been persuaded to sing in a café. To make it easier to remember the words of the song, he wrote them down on his shirt-cuffs. Unfortunately the cuffs were detachable and Charlie lost them; so he was forced to improvise. This is what he sang:

Se Bella pew satoré, je notre so katoré,
Je notre qui kavoré, je la ku la qui kwa!
La spinash or le busho, cigaretto toto bello,
Ce rakish spagoletto, so la tu, la tu, la twa!
Senora pe le finah, voulez-vous la taximeter,
La zionta sur le tita, tu le tu le tu le waah!

And on and on, complete nonsense. It was fitting that these were the first and the last words the Tramp ever spoke.

Another reason why Charlie made so few films during this time was because his popularity began to decline. Not that people thought his films weren't good any longer: it was just that America was going through a period when everyone was terrified of Communists, and for some reason Charlie was suspected of being one. America prided itself on being 'the land of opportunity', a country in which anyone could become President, in which hard work would be rewarded. The Red Menace — as the Communists were called — believed in a society of equals, one which was opposed to individuality, to free enterprise, to wealth, property — in effect, all that America stood for. However Charlie loved his adopted country for exactly those things it was proud of — the opportunities it provided, the limitless scope for those with energy, vision, and ambition. But the fear of the Red Menace was so strong that Charlie's concern with social issues was treated as evidence against him. The fact that he criticised some of the injustices he saw was read as a total condemnation of the American way of life. He was accused of having joined the Communist Party, and this to the Americans was one of the most serious crimes anybody could be guilty of.

After the Second World War Charlie's problem reached a crisis. The US government became totally hysterical about the Red Menace and Charlie was hounded and persecuted for years, in every possible way. The American people, who had once loved him so much, turned completely against him. One of the accusations against Charlie was that he had never become an American citizen, and that therefore his loyalty was suspect. Charlie had never thought of changing his nationality. He was proud of being English; nevertheless he had given so much to American life.

In 1952, exhausted by the battle, Charlie decided to take a holiday in Europe. The American government saw its chance to get rid of him, and on September 17, when Charlie was on board ship, he received a telegram from the Immigration Department. It forbade him to return to the United States.

Charlie was almost destroyed by this. He couldn't understand what he had done to deserve such treatment. Just a brief lifetime ago he had been a hero. Exiled from his chosen home he tried to establish a new one in a little town in Switzerland.

His exile brought screams of protest from all over the world. Thousands of influential people gave Charlie their support and tried to get the US government to alter its decision, but in vain. Charles Spencer Chaplin faded quietly into retirement. It was a bitter end to a phenomenal career.

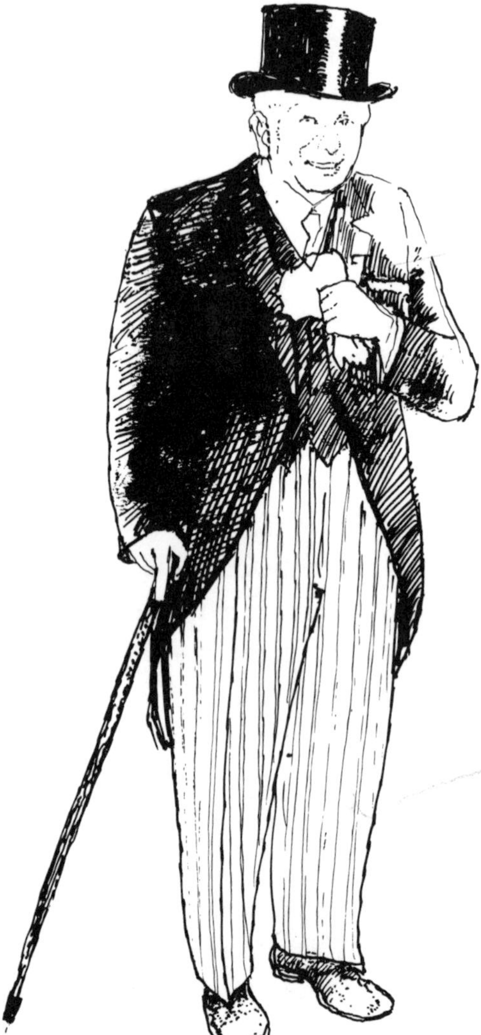

12 The Tramp Meets the Queen

Even the most painful wound heals. The American people got over their terror of Communists, and they were agonized by what they had done to such a great man. In 1971 Charlie received a special award for his films and he was made a Commander of the Legion of Honor — one of the highest decorations anyone can receive. America was anxious to make amends for its treatment of him, and in 1972 he was invited to the States to receive a special Oscar — the most distinguished film award in the world — for his services to the art of filmmaking. Charlie cried when he received this. Quite simply, he said, 'It surpasses everything.'

The recognition of Charlie's incredible contribution to the world of entertainment didn't end there. In 1975 Queen Elizabeth II knighted him. Charlie Chaplin, the Tramp, was now Sir Charles Spencer Chaplin, a Knight Commander of the British Empire.

And what of the Tramp?

Charlie Chaplin died on Christmas Day 1977. However, the Tramp, a gentleman, a poet, a dreamer,

a lonely fellow, always hopeful of romance and adventure . . . . he is immortal. He is the symbol of independence, the destroyer of dullness and pain. He is enchantment and joy, pleasure and sadness —
And we will always love him.

921 CHA   Sacranie, Ra
          Charlie Cha

DATE	BORROWER'S NAME
NOV 3	Ken Williams
NOV 21	Ken Williams
DEC 8	Phyllis Hayden
OCT 12	Joe Farler 503
OCT 26	Ralph Thompson 505